# HEADLINE NEWS

# HEADLINE NEWS

## JOHN DEMING

INDOLENT BOOKS

Cover art: Pete Wood & Pheanny Phen
Cover drawing and section drawings: Pete Wood
Book design: Nieves Guerra

Published by Indolent Books,
an imprint of Indolent Arts Foundation, Inc.
www.indolentbooks.com
Brooklyn, New York
ISBN: 978-1-945023-10-1

# CONTENTS

## 1

# 2

# 3

# 1

"i don't know anything. & neither do you."

—Frank Ocean, Twitter profile

## WITH SADNESS COMES ACCURACY; WITH HAPPINESS, FALSE MEMORY

so all my digital passwords
are based on personal tragedy

I remember your saddest expressions
I love how little rebels rebel

you put red streaks in your hair
after trying to kill yourself

all over America they're sadder
than their circumstances would suggest

the editors are read more than the reporters
because most people just read the headlines

NO CHARGES FOR WILSON
ARSON, RIOTING ERUPT IN FERGUSON
teenage atheists of the world unite

what it means to care seriously about nothing
America in love with its snipers

now everything is impulse
so everything's plausible
even likely

the loneliness
departed with
the headlines

TAN MOM: I DON'T CARE
WHAT YOU THINK

now we're blessed and beyond
beginning the evening

the sun and
sky blonde wine
and pink

break up the matter
slake like rain

BEARDED MEN CAUSE BRIDGE CLOSURE

bearded and crazy

unilaterally
what matters is
that they were bearded
and why

I'm feeling weirder
and clearer tonight

why must I be a teenager
I have ISIS on my face
it's time for a teenage rebellion
time for the iPhone X

J.D. SALINGER'S HOLDEN CAULFIELD AGING GRACELESSY
I tried to perform in one style at one clip
started taking pills and now I'm counting every breath

in the five-way Dyckman intersection
her face is everywhere
it's happening again

all day today an infinity of cows
computing flat-
footed and
grazing

MALIKI LEAVES WITH NO GUNS BLAZING

naked with back arched
your adjustments are amazing

I find this hotel off the highway
more sacred than last night's
you're just as crazy

what is my relationship with your god
what is my relationship with your media

the man with the black ski mask
the flashy blade in his hand
the man with the orange hat

INSIDE THE REPUBLICAN PARTY'S
DESPERATE MISSION TO STOP MR. TRUMP

compromising one's fears like putting
on an orange
hat

I last saw you increduling
my Aspirin my everything

it's late in the morning and I'm talking to the dead
the web on my radiator is interwoven and unending

snow tumbles in thickets
it's overreaching now

BOKO HARAM RELEASES SHOCKING IMAGES
OF CHILD SOLDIER TRAINING CAMP

in lateral shifts the same basic world war
wall to wall fleets of undead

N. KOREA: UNICORNS
ONCE EXISTED

I know
I've seen the tapestries

placid doesn't
know what
capture means

unicorn encircled
by a small pink fence
bleeding into flowers

if you don't assume
the zeitgeist then
you can't
evaporate

DILLS'
WINE
NOTES:
2001
FRANCISCAN
CABERNET

## CLAIRE DANES DEBUTS RED HAIR, TALKS MEETING OBAMA ON 'LATE SHOW'

I'm never not going to be
Angela Chase sitting on her bed

listening to the Cranberries'
"Dreams" then her mom comes in

and turns it down
Angela says just turn it off

Patty replies no
I like it

at the end of year party you
can talk about plans for the summer
what is your opinion on the use of ellipses in emails

we live in a cynical world and we work
in a business of tough competitors
I will be who I will be
concealed weapons are a virtue
what addictions do you think are ahead of you

TOUT EST PARDONNÉ
spoon a church and change headlines

oblivion
entered the world
and started nursing

in the name of god the giver of love the giver of mercy
SOMEONE BEAT US TO ALLAH

quoth the penguin
I know what to do
with this cigarette
but not when it's
gone

MISSING BABY FOUND IN TOTE BAG
pick him up at coat check

at what
do you I
wonder look
around

what's
happening
to us one at
a time

## HOW MUSIC THERAPY HELPS IN THE GRIEVING PROCESS

enough people
you know die
around

you over the years
you care less about
dying yourself

## 10 NEARLY PERFECT MOVIES, AND WHAT THEY CAN TELL US ABOUT STORYTELLING

movies actually make people cry
sometimes in a wedding scene playing Pachelbel's Canon
which they'll force you to meditate to
in every boring divorced kids group

which my aunt listened to driving
to the hospital when her husband was dying of cancer
he survived and a decade later
we became very close friends
I have a lot of gratitude for this

I'm praying for rain
I'm praying for surf
major human conflicts
are all about turf
I know I'm playing
nothing then I know
nothing is worse
NJ TAKES 3RD PLACE NATIONWIDE
FOR PEOPLE WHO LIKE
TO CURSE

### ONE: VOTERS APPROVE
### LOCAL OPTION BUDGET MEASURE

I don't really have passion for budgeting
look who's elegiac teenage and afraid

dude in commercial buys car
jumps for pleasure

on screensaver an airborne salmon that will enter
a bear's open mouth

that look
again on the fish's face

## VIN DIESEL VISITS PAUL WALKER GRAVE SITE

I needed to know for sure
now I do

we both said we were leaving
this life behind

I'll leave
it's important and so should you

I wish you could see
the world right now

I wish I could see it you're right

the news is the newest
or stimuli

installed
and bled right out

while I'm all my own
crepuscular head
MARIJUANA

LEGALIZATION
VOTE MAKES
ALASKA BALLOT

the space between freezing and melting
squeezed out on both sides

distance from the sun
I left my Nutrament at home

I'm trying to get paid
trying to get greased

you're dirty the moment
you take money for a job

REAL-LIFE HERO ADAM HARTSWICK
SHARES STORY OF SURVIVAL, RESOLVE

3 MEDICAL MARVELS SAVING LIVES
they'll be outdated
just as fast
you watch

the wheelbarrow
also was a tech
revolution

you can only save
lives for so
long

shit-talking mushrooms
scene on a plane

UK SHOWS INTEREST IN BUYING ANOTHER
C-17

the assembly line is closing
the royal air force is blessed

the moon just lightens
the specked noses of sika deer

each eating
sedges and grass

## ZOMBIE FACES: WHY ARE WE AFRAID OF THEM?

it's nothing at all if you don't pray to them
stories fold away
mulch
digital dirt
someone might have found them
if they proved somehow to be worth
more than the litany of stories
that replaces them

# 2

"The National Institute of Mental Health estimates that more than fourteen million Americans suffer from major depression every year, and more than three million suffer from minor depression (whose symptoms are milder but last longer than two years). Greenberg thinks that numbers like these are ridiculous—not because people aren't depressed but because, in most cases, their depression is not a mental illness. It's a sane response to a crazy world."

—Louis Menand, *The New Yorker,* March 1, 2010

blissful and beat
the whole car ride
ADDICTION TREATMENT

WITH A DARK SIDE
it's all dark side
that's what the song said

it'll prove to itself
it can still have you
and walk off again

I'm out of ideas and I hate conflict

WEBSITE TRACKS
BLACK FRIDAY DEATHS

these look like solid deals to me
silk flatscreen

how it feels to me
the determined unfolding

of all my intentions
into blossom

and practically
healing me

## A DAY IN THE LIFE OF THE WORLD'S BUSIEST AIRPORT

let down and hanging around
that's what it's here for

I'll drug
my own blood
in the bathroom

and pretty much
love every gate
where it leads

## HI. MY NAME IS KATY AND I'M A GRATEFUL ALCOHOLIC

I'd start on having babies
but I'm terrified of colic

I need some time to think
I think that's probably worthful

how a bubble in a
beer could be so

many perfect
circles

that terrible person
just screamed
I hate my kids

PROSECUTOR: POPE FACES MAFIA 'RISK'

drunken nothing worth
looking at is better than
the sky

how could my brass
crooked ashtray
I'll find it

don't know anyone very well
it's impossible to think
then a surge of hope from where the neck
angles into the spine
COMING BACK FROM THE BRINK

we're fostering hysteria
for the pablum
down the hall
there's a proxy war in Syria
a sound in every wall

had an MRI of my brainstem
had a brainstem I didn't build
had a building on my block that was way overpriced
had mice in my walls in my head

'HAD MY EYE ON HIS RECORD'—SHAKIB
don't know for sure who Shakib is

it's all a great deception
it's all Tania Head
Gretchen there are forces behind our walls
in the generic sense free will

longhorn skull over a fireplace
bulletthole between the eyeholes
and as big as them

that's the way that I feel
when I wake up
I'm a citizen

it's never been a dry vote
everyone's recidivists

all various kinds of addicts
MARCO RUBIO'S PROBLEM ISN'T WHAT YOU THINK IT IS

little tiny Xanax
swimming down a throat
in this way it looks like a tadpole
in this way it runs like a goat
ANGER: AS AMERICAN AS APPLE PIE
in this way it looks like a fear
someone starts smoking
someone turns into leaves
hard times for a cockroach
for old chandeliers

let me reintroduce myself
I think everything everyone else

has ever thought
it's gotten boring

I'm getting bitter now
blue-eyed and yawning

I'd much rather be part
of an angry majority

TODDLERS DETECT EMOTION,
CHANGE BEHAVIOR ACCORDINGLY

there was an earthquake
and the chandelier
fell on the roast

ROBIN WILLIAMS' DEATH RULED SUICIDE

this room is filled with pretty ghosts

I need you to talk to you please
answer your texts
pick up your fucking phone

it's nothing I've resigned myself
to dying upended alone

## BAFFLING 400,000-
## YEAR-OLD CLUE
## TO HUMAN ORIGINS

save yourself get part of your head
around mortal blues someone cue the horns again
Easter is about rabbits and I'm born again
what gorgeous corporate teasing

let's chain-smoke on the fire escape
and fall in love again
it'll be easy

I'm plasticene
I'm plastic
my debts exceed
my assets

got the need and latitude
for depression medication

TOP DOC: MEDIA BIAS
ON ANTIDEPRESSANTS
'ASTOUNDING'

amazing

no time to be depressed
I'm surviving and I'm sleeping
AUTISM RISK MAY BE LINKED TO MOTHER'S DEPRESSION,
NOT MEDICATION
comfort of any kind means
devastation or further planning

trusting anyone is alien
next a torrent of infatuation so damning
government cancer cells silos and skies

like it's practicing routine capitalism
it needs to expand to survive

## ANTIDEPRESSANT USE ON THE RISE IN RICH COUNTRIES, OECD FINDS

I had to kill a fly by the window
almost always I let them survive

I've been given
the power of pardon

and lived the same
thoughts for a while

now I'm in the air with maybe seconds left
and a billion blazing eyes

## BEAUTY'S BRIDGE PLUNGE

Ashley's jewelry line was called Missfits
she made them by hand

the way you feel is not an illusion
there is always underlying form
I sit at a keyboard night after night committing fraud
thin string white stone orchid jewel black ball

and don't you all feel guilty

yes they do
your bracelets are beautiful

man in commercial
hugging a van
it's not at all personal
I'm drunk as Gauguin
I'm fading like Van Gogh
I'm boosted now I'm versatile
you've got to leave me alone tonight
I'm scared and alone with a verse in my head
10 THINGS I LOVED ABOUT PARIS
the worst I forget

it means you know somewhere
there's a sound for what you feel
and just in time
doesn't need to be perfect
or you could read or get eaten by a river
IT STARTS WITH A CLEAR SENSE OF PERSONAL PURPOSE
few levels of misery
aren't corroborated by language or music
but they're there I'm afraid
inside cages with purpose

### ARCTIC WOLF PUPS TO BECOME WILDLIFE CENTER 'WOLF AMBASSADORS'

faces filling arenas fixed on warm lighted centers
just where our dead ought to sit

in one stadium they watch and interpret
applaud each of us our obvious ends
we pattern into them and watch the rest

formless heroes living daily against their deaths
with modest hope caged let it pace
apologize like an angry god
it cannot leave

clouds of mold
flat on the ceiling
now they're spinning
around my head
when did this
become my
bathroom when
did this become my head

4000 DEAD IN TACLOBAN
ALONE it's in my head

I forget what we're talking about
in the middle of the conversation

forget why I left one chamber
and entered another chamber

few things are as inevitable
as mental deterioration

HOT ON THE TRAIL
OF THE UNIVERSE'S DARKEST SECRET

I don't know anyone very well
I like being alone on the weekend

what would Frasier Crane do
he'd put this shit away
KELSEY GRAMMER OPENS UP
ABOUT HIS LOVE AFFAIR WITH COCAINE
he wanted to live a new life
new lives are not that great

I'm in the mood for love
I'm in the mood for things
what would Sideshow Bob do
I love it when he sings

IS SOCIAL MEDIA MAKING YOU
SOULLESS?
I don't know
your eyes
break
like
forests
and suddenly
darkening
with snow

4 ARRESTED IN CONNECTION WITH HOFFMAN DRUGS

get me more
or let real
loose I get to
guarding my
own floors

every time I am
alone I get to
pardon my
old form

# 3

"And I began to see her by watching certain people, by watching for her, watching for my character...And I began to see that there would be very small things she would do and very peculiar things that she would say to reveal her torment. I began to see that this is what we all do, all of the time, all of us, including you and me. That whatever is really driving us is what can never, never, never be hidden and is there to see if someone wants to see it."

—James Baldwin, "Words of a Native Son"

I wake only in the middle of crisis
the absolute power of ISIS
the loudest blast yet in the brightest
of all probable worlds
spills contumely and politeness

15 QUESTIONS
ABOUT THE CHALLENGE
OF FINDING
MR. RIGHTEOUS
you know I know no one likes this

so why are you still writing it

a slight crease alone it
houses the dead

POPE FRANCIS, LEAVE
THESE NUNS ALONE!

only it's time to lead mouse
to bread

Crystal said she doesn't like Ambien
because a giant eye closes
around her head

generalized American
your fears are justified

the Titanic will always be sinking
no one knows you were alive

maybe the premise this fact even matters
promotes such unmerciful anxiety

REPUBLICAN CAMPAIGN ADS
FEAR-MONGERING OVER ISIS THREAT

judge each other
I trust you don't lie to me

## DON'T BLAME METEOROLOGISTS FOR THE SOUTH'S TERRIBLE RESPONSE TO SNOW

don't blame them at all

I mean keeping them
out of all of it

I mean it obsequiously
there's life past the shorelines

speckled life
breathing halibut

now watch me establish my caliphate
your maps are officially useless

grown indefensibly old
but still arming bridges for Halliburton

all sneering and strategy
all toothless

DICK CHENEY WAS LYING ABOUT TORTURE

scatter you aphids
it's late and I'm
doing this

you can be an egomaniac
but have no self confidence

I spent more
and took a train
that fell apart
I'm blaming communists

that's not recalcitrance
just a priori awareness of
EVERYTHING,

AND OUR PROBLEM WITH IT

ISIS FLAG FLOWN AT TUNISIA SOCCER MATCH

the late stages as always
threaded back to the open
I hate cages and love anthrax
it's a strangler fig
choking

duplicitous misunderstood
underestimated and chosen
carving wooden necks
with one complete and open motive

strict karma is a ridiculous idea
generalized karma is not
discipline comes from suffering
suffering comes from god
god's beyond the world of forms
forms are all we've got
I'm awfully thankful
for my form right now NASA:
WATER WORLDS OF OUR SOLAR SYSTEM
AND BEYOND

belief in the destiny of values
means community and fear

SCREENING FOR MENTAL HEALTH ISSUES
MAY NOT GUARANTEE CARE

when there is thunder
my schnauzer gets scared

the emotional lives of penguins
our emotional lives in dreams

birds fed by dreams and the holes they leave
as with unimpaired meteor streams

MAYOR PRAISES MARCH
governor chastises April

I'm not in a very good mood
fucked up the zippers on two of my staples
on television we all know just what happens
to most of the good-intentioned and capable

it's the will to do it
the thought you thought you could
I worship money
don't judge fucking shame on you

no no fuck that
money is a means not an end
the gospel of acknowledging ignorance first
the gospel of empathy is dead
I love you but don't trust you
I love a capital-seeking drone
learn real well how to stroke yourself
measure by measure of thought
YES, THE KOCH BROTHERS REALLY ARE THAT EVIL
fuck their accomplices too

if I wanted more Twitter followers I would tweet more
Google famous Simpsons lines Seymour

he's ruined more school assemblies
than the sun in the northern window

I see you're trembling I love you
I misplaced my thinking
my self-destructive streak was over completely and then
    it wasn't

FOX NEWS SEES PROFIT AND VIEWERSHIP RISE,

CABLE NEWS COMPETITION
DOESN'T

## CONSPIRACY THEORIES:
## WHY WE BELIEVE THE UNBELIEVABLE

people
need
to
stop
having
ideas
about
people

a comically ambitious criticism
of style over substance

what luck to get to witness
make lists of what's
always left dangling and repugnant

YOUNG MIDTERM-ELECTION VOTERS

go on

WILL LIKELY BE
VOTING FOR
REPUBLICANS

head tilted back
on a mustard couch

marsala button-down
shirt no

pocket that's a film
crew in my head

SOUND SYSTEM SIMULATES
A ROCKET BLAST,
WOULD KILL YOU
JUST AS DEAD

it occurs to me
America
I'm talking to myself

it occurs to me I'm earth wind fire
and problems with my health

I am the world
then wake up world
we are the world we are the pilgrims

THE REPUBLICAN ART OF DENIAL
it seems knowingness can kill you

McNulty has dinner with Terry
says he voted neither Bush nor Kerry

what else
can you do
leave it alone
like that forsythia

it's like it never
connects

I.S. EXPANDS
IN LIBYA

there's violet on her eyelid
and a thin black line

it's getting quiet on the plane
the pilot's still doing his job

I saw him with a cup of coffee
and a spent banana peel

INSIDE DECEMBER
*VOGUE*

what's he think about
up here

space between one's skull and one's knowing what to do
space between my toe and the toe of my shoe

FEED YOUR
HUNGRY BABIES,
POPE TELLS MOTHERS
IN SISTINE CHAPEL

on the ceiling we're barely a fingertip
from god
these things obviously
will  happen

I purchased all my groceries
my student loans aren't paid

a mendicant is a beggar
opprobrium means public shame

a sepulcher is a burial chamber
to supplicate is to beg

hirsute means furry or hairy
a mendicant supplicates

LETTER: WAKE UP AMERICA,
BEFORE IT IS TOO LATE

she'll always be dead in the ground like that
earth will be a pellet of hail

the status quo discreetly saves your life at that point
I mean indirectly like it always did

oh please keep me alive one more day
o who am I saying that to whom

has more power over that than me
THERE'S NO GOD BUT ALLAH, NO LANGUAGE BUT URDU

if I just believe in context
what's the first thing I should do

JAMES BALDWIN'S PARIS

I've been failing to write a character
all I've ever really wanted is oblivion
truth covered in security

NYC A train sometimes one inhabits them
or sometimes
barely sees them
with knowingness the greatest threat there is to human
        freedom
and knowing this as just another knowingness
conceded

WORLD'S FIRST BIRTH FROM TRANSPLANTED WOMB
one commenter wants the doctor imprisoned

me I was born
by Caesarean Section
I'm still frightened by the sound of an incision

the rational ethics of listening well
and defending only researched opinions

should be obvious at this point
it's all the dead have left us with
that and their pretty disappearance

okay so the worst has happened
someone build a fire

TRUMP TRIUMPHS
I still have my Duane Reade
Rewards card I'll be fine

after all it's still just the rest of the world and you

some hundred million others wondering
how to overcome extreme
sadness
what to do

# NOTES

All items in small caps are actual headlines taken from print and digital media.

"at the end of year party you" contains a line from the movie *Jerry Maguire*

"10 NEARLY PERFECT MOVIES..." IS FOR ROCCO

"VIN DIESEL VISITS PAUL WALKER GRAVE SITE" contains lines from one of *The Fast and the Furious* movies

"A DAY IN THE LIFE OF THE WORLD'S" contains a line from Radiohead's "Let Down"

"BEAUTY'S BRIDGE PLUNGE" is for Ashley Riggitano, I.M.

"belief in the destiny of values" references John Ashbery's "Self-Portrait in a Convex Mirror"

"MAYOR PRAISES MARCH" references John Berryman's "Dream Song 1" "if I wanted more Twitter followers I would tweet more" copies a line from *The Simpsons* episode "The Ned-Liest Catch"

"it occurs to me" references Allen Ginsberg's "America"

"JAMES BALDWIN'S PARIS" contains a line from Nirvana's "Lounge Act"

# ACKNOWLEDGMENTS

Thanks to the editors of these journals for publishing these selections, sometimes in earlier versions:

*BOAAT*: "the news is the newest," "if you don't assume," "head tilted back"

*Boston Review*: "ARCTIC WOLF PUPS…"

*A Dozen Nothing*: "WITH SADNESS COMES ACCURACY," "why must I be a teenager," "what is my relationship with your god," "CLAIRE DANES DEBUTS RED HAIR," "ZOMBIE FACES: WHY ARE WE," "blissful and beat," "WEBSITE TRACKS," "what would Frasier Crane do," "4 ARRESTED IN CONNECTION WITH HOFFMAN DRUGS," "DON'T BLAME METEOROLOGISTS," "now watch me establish my caliphate," "a comically ambitious criticism," "McNulty has dinner with Terry," "I purchased all my groceries," "she'll always be dead in the ground like that," "WORLD'S FIRST BIRTH FROM TRANSPLANTED WOMB," "okay so the worst has happened"

*Map Literary*: "I'm praying for rain," "shit-talking mushrooms," "A DAY IN THE LIFE OF THE WORLD'S," "HI. MY NAME IS KATY," "that terrible person," "don't know anyone very well," "longhorn skull over a fireplace," "clouds of mold," "I forget what we're talking about"

*Omniverse*: "it means you know somewhere," "IS SOCIAL MEDIA MAKING YOU," "strict karma is a ridiculous idea," "belief in the destiny of values," "it occurs to me," "space between one's skull," "JAMES BALDWIN'S PARIS"

*Ostrich Review*: "ANTIDEPRESSANT USE ON THE RISE," "BEAUTY'S BRIDGE PLUNGE," "man in commercial," "there was an earthquake"

*Valley Voices*: "the loneliness," "break up the matter," "MISSING BABY FOUND IT TOTE BAG," "N. KOREA: UNICORNS," "LINCOLN'S LESSONS," "HOW MUSIC," "I wake only in the middle of crisis," "so why are you still writing it"

This book is dedicated to my parents, Mary Wood-Gauthier and Len Deming.

I also owe a major debt to the following people and organizations who have supported me and my writing over the years: Melinda Wilson, Jim Wood, Joanne Wood, Matthew Yeager, Graeme Bezanson, Mark

Bibbins, David Lehman, Rosebud ben-Oni, Michael Broder, Jason Schneiderman, Michael J. Wilson, James Kimbrell, Mekeel McBride, Charles Simic, D.A. Powell, Rae Armantrout, Clark Knowles, Jonathan Wells, Dana Levin, Christopher Salerno, Erin Belieu, Lysa James, Timothy Donnelly, Rebecca Wolff, Shane McCrae, John Parras, Angela Ball, Rusty Morrison, Ken Keegan, Timothy Welsh, Sandra Simonds, Matt Soucy, Matthew Maynard, Komo Ananda, Adam Trull, Seth Graves, Peter Longofono, Devin Kelly, Erin Lynn, Robert Polito, Prageeta Sharma, Kate Angus, Ali Power, Nicholas Adamski, Stephanie Berger, Pete Miller, Jeff Sirkin, Angela Ball, Brett Fletcher Lauer, Michael Klein, Nico Vassilakis, Crystal Curry, the Port Townsend Writers Conference, The New York City Poetry Festival, and everyone who has ever been involved with *Coldfront.*

I.M. Liam Rector, "a few years/To play around..."

Bestpoetalive.com
Coldfrontmag.com
Indolentbooks.com

# ABOUT THE AUTHOR

**John Deming** has published poems and articles in *Boston Review, Salon, Fence, New Orleans Review, A Public Space, Critical Studies in Men's Fashion,* and elsewhere. He is Editor in Chief of *Coldfront* and lives in New York City, where he directs the Writing Center at LIM College and co-curates KGB Monday Night Poetry in the East Village.

# ABOUT INDOLENT BOOKS

Indolent Books is a small independent poetry press founded in 2015 and operating in Brooklyn. Indolent champions innovative, provocative, risky poems and the poets who write them, especially voices from underrepresented communities including but not limited to poets over 50 as well as poets who are gay, lesbian, bisexual, transgender, gender nonconforming, queer, or nonwhite.

www.ingramcontent.com/pod-product-compliance
Lightning Source LLC
Chambersburg PA
CBHW020035120526
44588CB00031B/697
* 9 7 8 1 9 4 5 0 2 3 1 0 1 *